To Christopher and family.
With love from Mother.
        Sept. 27th, 2000.

ANCHOR BOOKS

PERFECT PETS

Edited by

Steve Twelvetree

First published in Great Britain in 2000 by
ANCHOR BOOKS
Remus House,
Coltsfoot Drive,
Woodston,
Peterborough, PE2 9JX
Telephone (01733) 898102

HB ISBN 1 85930 890 2
SB ISBN 1 85930 895 3

FOREWORD

A book of tales to be truly treasured, *Perfect Pets* contains humorous and heartfelt verse which reflects the love and affection which we flourish on our pets, and the companionship and dedication they offer us in return - truly becoming our faithful friends.

With tales of fat cats, catnaps, mischievous mice and furry ferrets, this new anthology of verse provides an inspirational insight into the 'perfect pets' we share our lives with.

A delightful book for the animal lovers amongst us which you'll truly enjoy reading time and time again.

Steve Twelvetree
Editor

CONTENTS

THE CAT

Jade stones watch and stare
The fast rippling breath
Of a creature unaware
That a shadow is covering
The light of his life.

The rich intruder shows his twenty daggers
And pounds upon the victim
Piercing the skin silently.
Dropping his bottom jaw
Grips the creature, turns and goes.

Christine Russell

TRUDIE

A scared and shaking little pup
I couldn't wait to pick you up
To take you home
And calm yours fears
To share our lives for years and years

Your pedigree was very short
But love like yours could not be bought
With one blue eye the other brown
I knew you were the best in town

We lived together for sixteen years
You cheered me up when I shed tears
You made me laugh, you kept me warm
Protected me from every harm

But you grew tired you needed sleep
And so my memories I'll keep
Of you my true and loyal friend
You'll be with me until my end

Jenny Smallwood

MY CAT

My cat is such a clever cat as he roams about the house,
He doesn't catch too many birds, but he often gets a mouse.
He isn't really ordin'ry like every other cat,
As nearly every afternoon he and I, we have a chat.

I first saw him twelve years ago in a great big cardboard box,
He was the smallest of the litter as he snuggled to some socks.
He raised his head, he meowed, he winked, he whispered 'I am yours,'
I picked him up and help him tight and answered 'Yes, of course!'

Well since that day he's done a lot, he talks to everyone he meets,
Be they walking down our footpath or walking down the streets.
But people never answer him, they don't seem to understand,
That our cat's a talking cat, the cleverest in the land.

He told me about a year ago a rugby match he'd played,
For a union team in London, with Carling he had stayed.
Of course, I didn't believe him, I said 'Not on your nelly!'
He nodded, winked and said 'Goodnight, watch News at Ten
                                          on telly.'

I watched the News at Ten that night read by a serious bloke,
He read about a war or two and to a politician spoke.
But as he read the sports' news, I was woken from a nap,
I'm certain that I heard him say, 'My cat wins England cap.'

James Cooke

MIAOW

We own two little ginger 'moggies'
Treacle and Toffee are their names,
They sit in the window and watch the 'doggies'
Going for 'walkies' down the lane.

They're full of mischief - and lots of fun
Doing many things they shouldn't,
Like climbing curtains and pulling them down!
And making us laugh - who wouldn't?

They chase each other fast and furious,
Then sharpen their claws on the chairs;
They explore every corner, being ever so curious
And everywhere's covered in hairs!

We make sure their food is always the best
Costing us plenty of lolly,
Then they pick out the best bits and leave all the rest
And lick out the tins for the jelly!

But then on an evening, the fire-glow all rosy,
We all snuggle up together,
A cat on each lap all dozy and cosy
Precious moments to remember forever.

Mary Gelder

IN MEMORY OF TABBY 1982-1999

In '82 a terrible storm brought you to our home,
Funny and gentle, soft and kind,
I never felt alone.
But the snow that came last April
Carved your name in wintry form,
I did not know that cold, soft bed
Had come to take you home.
Quietly you slipped away
Too far for me to go,
I wanted to pretend things were just the same
Before God sent the snow.
Two months passed and then he appeared,
This replica of you,
I pushed him aside, I pushed him away,
The hurt was just too new.
The family thought him charming,
But I am not so easily led,
So then why is he gazing at me so lovingly
From the bottom of my bed?

Dawn Jones

TAMMY GOES FOR TRAINING
(Puppy Walker)

You came when you were eight weeks old,
a cute, black Labrador.
You were just adorable,
I couldn't have loved you more.

You ate snails and flowers and frogs,
you'd love to play with other dogs.
We'd go for runs in Sutton Park
and go for long walks in the dark.
We'd do our training every day
and practise sit, down, wait and stay.
We'd go to town on a train
but get the bus back home again.
We've even been to swimming baths,
Tam, you've gave me lots of laughs.

Now you've gone for training,
the house is not the same.
I have a job believing
I won't see you again.
One day perhaps you'll qualify
and be a DfD.*
I hope you're placed with someone
who'll love you, just like me.
Maybe you'll change someone's life,
I really hope you do.
I'm proud that I have walked you,
so now it's up to you.

So God bless you little Tammy,
as you have hard work to do,
always remember, Tammy,
that I'll never forget you.

Linda Prescott

** DfD 'Dogs for the disabled' are specially trained from puppies to
assist disabled people with everyday tasks.*

HARVEY AND TESS

He's large and bouncy, loves company,
Follows you around constantly.
He's got a time clock in his head,
Knows when it's time to go out,
When it's time to be fed.
He loves his comforts, believe you me,
When I turn my back, he's on the settee.
He's very possessive of squeaky toys,
Chasing 'Mr Torchy' (a light) he really enjoys.
He presents you with gifts to welcome you home,
His lead, a shoe, the mobile phone.
Sings very well in a baritone key,
He's going on ten, acts if he's three.
When he strips the bed, he's a pain in the neck,
But never mind, what the heck!
He's one of us, part of the family,
Goes by the name of Handsome Harvey.

We can't keep her out of water,
She loves swimming in the sea,
Active and lively, a bundle of energy.
She's a proper madam, likes to sit upon your lap
Where she's quite contented to have a little nap.
She's very fond of carrots
And over pineapples she'll drool,
She gets a silly ten minutes
And acts like a fool.
If Harvey gets too boisterous
No nonsense will she take,
Although a lot smaller in size,
She puts him in his place.
She's funny and fickle, very often a pest,
A right little fuss pot,
Our dog Tess.

Sylvia Bevan

THE BROWN PONY

He looked longingly, stood with the other,
An adorable Yorkshire pup. He had a silky coat and big brown eyes
And a tail that wagged out of control.
But I'm allergic to pets, and to that sweet little guy.
He could never have me for his mother.

He stood wooden, poised amongst the rummage,
An erst proud steed. His brown coat was now time-worn,
And his mane only an ink-black fringe,
A red saddle, astride, expectantly borne
For his mount and a bridle for his manage.

Alone, he stood with his pink nostrils flaring
And a fixed monocular gaze on the trade.
I was browsing close by when he spotted me
And toppled to draw my attention. He laid
On his side, mute, his red and black wheels turning.

I hurried to help him and set him upright.
I stroked his worn coat and his balding black mane,
Saw the dolorous look in his one good eye.
That's the moment - that gaze - when it became plain
I was won, we were bound; he was mine from that night.

Donna Fitzsimmons

IT'S ONLY A HORSE

Oh people, do you not have sight,
To see me standing in such plight?
You look at me, but do not see, a horse,
Have you no pity, no remorse?

You who dash around this square,
You pass me by, hardly a stare,
You do not seem to see my plight,
Have you no heart, no eyes, no sight?

The sun beats down on bony haunch,
You pass me by, from your own lunch,
Bloated you pass, happy, gay,
I get no water, shade or hay.

I stand in dusty, polluted square,
The odd tourist stops, gives me a stare,
My coat is dirty, black as coal,
But even a horse has dreams, a soul.

To you I lay my dreams so bare,
You know I once was a young white mare,
Who played and gambolled on parched land,
And then you humans took a hand!

I have heard of lands with fields of green,
Where horses eat their fill and dream,
You thank your God, for oh such peace,
I ask that same God for release.

So here I stand, head down, no hope,
Dirty, with each day I cope,
So if there is a God above,
Then let me die, and meet your love.

J Deekes

MY FRIEND

He was tall, fair and handsome
Patient, true and kind
And when life's problems got me down
No better friend I'd find.

But though his sight began to fail
His hearing not so good,
He'd faithfully watch over his sick master
And every day at half past four, lie in wait for me.

Alas, finally arthritis attacked his bones
And he bravely struggled to welcome me home.
We went for walks together, very slowly, guiding him
Where once he used to run and play.

But sadly, I knew the day had come
When we would have to part.
14 years a faithful friend
No more could be allowed to suffer so much pain.

So, he was given his last cuddle
And allowed to die with dignity,
Now the house seems quiet, no longer he's stood at the door
There's just memories of a very special canine friend.

Beryl Ellis

UNTITLED

Our seven pets
We love to bits
Our Holly and Angel can do tricks
Although they cost a lot of money
They really are so funny
So get a pet and give it love
And never part with it
And you will see just
How happy you
Will be

Our Angel is a pom
Our Holly looks like a lamb
Our Beth is like a boy
Our four cats sure do try
To eat us out of house and home
But I bet they won't roam
So love your pets as they love you
And you will never be alone

Jenny Reader

ODE TO A FURRY NEWFOUNDLAND

You're everywhere I look,
especially when I cook.
Constantly floating around our home,
flying freely, always on the roam.

I'm talking about newfie fur,
not only the bain of my life,
but also that of my wife!

In the fridge, in the cupboard,
under the stairs.
In ones and threes,
often in pairs.

Brush it, comb it, fur still appears,
under the cushions, behind my ears!

Clogs up the hoover, clogs up the sink,
one more blocked drain and I think I'll see pink.

But with those deep soulful eyes,
who could resist.
Oh, that reminds me, to include dust bags on the shopping list.

But, when all's said and done, we love her dearly,
the pleasure she brings, shows quite clearly.
And for another breed of dog, we wouldn't swop,
even when, on wet days,
she looks just like a mop!

Alison Jones

THREE PLUS TWO

When we were 'young and foolish' we ran away
To a country idyll under the romantic hill,
Strewing love prodigally, adopting three starving country cats
Which slept in grocery boxes in the hall - I see them still.

As we returned at night up the dark lane they ran
Ecstatically to meet us, tails high, singing their joy,
Came in for the warm evening, fed, purred, settled,
Sharing our retreat from the world's ploy.

Then our dreams broke up, broke part of us and wreckage
Soured the rural scene awhile and peace fled.
It was long ago: the three soft, affectionate hearts,
Like others, people, faces, must be long dead.

Two more, in peril, knocked at my different door,
The male stupid (like me) but meaning well, the woman bright,
Grateful and loving, wanting (like all) shelter and rest,
Commonplace, but sometimes the commonplace is right.

And so the past came back, my need, perhaps, as theirs.
And they too and I, will go, but where to? - where?
Like the three, either to nothing, or to something strange
And wonderful, where two times meet, when love is there.

The trifling tasks of love are so familiar and their pleasure
At being taken in, familiar too and like the old,
As if they came to say 'The others sent us.'
There is only one story to be told, to be told.

Roy Stevens

TEN TOR CHECKER

When through the mist
You hear a bark
And see a shadow on the moor
Then you will know
It's only Dando
Still at his checkpoint on the Tor.

Joan Spurling

WHAT AM I?

I am a little friend
So small and sweet
My name is Toffee
With four little feet
I have two pouches
To store my food
Which I sit and eat
When in the mood
I take my exercise
In my ball
And I hope I do not fall
My nose it twitches
Up and down
And on my wheel
I go round and round
Guess what I am?

Suzann J Taylor

LITTLE OLD DOG MIKE

Little old dog who's deaf and blind
children grown up, he's left behind
he doesn't wag his tail no more
at times can't even find our door
looks at a bone as much to say
I think I'm out of luck today
a bone I used to love to chew
but now it's something I can't do
I'm just toothless but as a pup
two seconds I would chew it up
I have no teeth and I can't see
in fact I can't scratch a flee
at bath times now I can't protest
I just sit there and do my best
I make a face as much to say
let me out now I'm OK
I've been a Romeo in my time
and seen a lot of pups of mine
middle of the night now I try to roam
but two minutes later I'm back home
and then I cry at the wrong door
something I never did before
I snore and make wind like an old man
but really I'm just glad I can
I'm old now, yes I'm seventeen
so treat me nice and don't be mean
one day I'll just not be around
you'll cry and put me underground
if you get another dog you like
please be kind don't call it Mike

A Carter

MY BEST FRIEND

My best friend wears a coat of fur,
His eyes shine like the sun.
He likes to sleep in his favourite chair,
Oblivious of everyone.

He likes to go out hunting,
Sometimes he climbs a tree.
And then he comes home proudly,
With a present just for me.

We often sit together,
In quiet company.
He always knows when I am sad,
And tries to comfort me.

He knows I love him dearly,
There is no doubt of that.
I would not be without him,
My best friend is my cat.

Barbara Smith

OUR TETHERED, FEATHERED FRIEND

Cluck, cluck, cluck
Familiar to us all this chicken sound
Eggs roll out in numerous quantity
Awaiting mouths at breakfast time
The farmers' yard, a happy scene
Obscuring death behind closed doors
The chicken slaughtered makes his way
To the chicken shed at the end of the lane
Christmas comes and we all expect
A drum or two of this supple white flesh
We gorge our way to the calcium cavern
Stripping the chick of its once manoeuvrable flesh
Un-undignified end for our egg-producing
Tethered, feathered friend.

David Clarke

PEPPER

Small legs that run with amazing speed;
Teeth so determined to chew on the lead;
Small dash of orange above each bright, brown eye
Like eyebrows raised in constant surprise.

Sausage-shaped body - a subject of mirth
A mixture of colours round your ample girth,
Browns, blacks and orange - a beautiful sight
And, in the middle - one strand of white.

Fanned tail dancing in graceful art
Undercoat matted with dried grass and clart
How risky, when raining, to give you a hug
For nobody wants a handful of slug!

When groomed you're a Dachshund fit for a queen
Strutting around so proud to be seen.
To the fore - head held high - the world is yours
To the rear - one would think you were wearing plus-fours!

Long ears more suited to rabbit or hare
Flap as you run, like a bird in the air.
From your chest comes a noise like the chug of a train
While your body tries hard to keep pace with your brain.

Your gentle ways - oh how they beguile!
Each look that you give is just like a smile
So timid with strangers - not privy to see
To side of your nature shown daily to me.

There's no darkness in you, just sweetness and light.
If people were like you there'd be no need to fight.
When I'm down and wondering what the future will be
A nudge from your nose says, 'You've still got me!'
Though a figure of fun to some you appear
You're the joy in my life - I'm so glad you're here!

G E Tate

BEN'S ADVENTURE

When Ben went for his walkies
One Monday afternoon
He wandered off a bit too far
It made Diana swoon

No sign of Ben at teatime
No sign of him for bed
He had them all demented
They thought that he was dead

Diana worried all night long
Where could that doggie be?
He's off on an adventure
And he's gone and missed his tea

A million 'phone calls later
That wandering mutt was found
Nice and snug and comfortable
In the doggie pound

Fifty-four pounds poorer
Diana took Ben home
To dream of his adventure
Never again to roam

L Curtis

PIP

I had a little dog called Pip
Who meant all the world to me
Now he has gone to doggie heaven above
The little dog who gave so much love

When my husband passed away
My life I could not see
But Pip looked at me as if to say
You know you've still got me

When it was time for walkies
He'd go stand by the door
With ears cocked back, his eyes alert
He couldn't ask for more

Through rain and hail, and snow and blow
He didn't give a jot
As long as he had his walkies
Down the lanes he'd trot

Then as he grew older
He wasn't quite as quick
But though he had gone slower
He didn't miss a trick

Then one day he nearly stopped
His little legs went weak
I tried to carry him in my arms
But help I had to seek

He tried to keep going for me
So brave up to the end
I knew I had to let him go
My dear old faithful friend

F Thompson

LITTLE MOTHER

We called her 'Little Mother' - she looked quite old and grey,
As long as I could remember she'd always been that way.
She seemed to smile when happy and frowned a lot when sad,
Sometimes she'd stay away all day - then we knew her mood was bad.
But she always liked a kind word, a smile, a nod, a wave,
A kiss, perhaps a cuddle towards the end of day.
Very little would upset her and we loved her funny ways,
A cat who loved attention - part of our family - here to stay.

P Sanders

ODE TO BORIS (A PET RAT WHO ONCE ESCAPED)
(Dedicated to Laura and Jennifer)

When your rat has got up and gone
Then, gosh, you really do know
The sweetest sun which once shone
Has departed and cold winds blow.

'Come home Boris,' shout the people;
Not a single dry eye in all the land,
From the lowest gutter to highest steeple,
Frozen ice-caps to parched Sahara sand.

Boris - a lovely, little friendly rat;
Cute, clever and great fun to be around,
AWOL - it's just as simple as that,
Believed to be partying about town.

Come home Boris!

Ian D Henery (Walsall)

UNTITLED

I have a cat, her name is Sam,
I cannot say how glad I am,
She came to stay in 84,
She is the one I adore.

Famannia Chantelle is her real name,
A chocolate Burmese, so very tame,
Her mum won prizes, a champion was she,
But Sam doesn't need rosettes for me.

So small with big gold eyes,
The voice of a baby, when it cries,
She eats so little, I have to say,
Trim, neat, immaculate in every way.

She has a visitor we call Black and White,
He comes to see her both day and night,
Friend or foe? We're not quite sure,
She shouts a lot and goes out the door.

She's semi retired and sleeps a lot,
Feeling weary as likely as not,
The birds know Sam is no threat,
But if she tried, she'd catch one yet.

She loves a fuss, a lovely pet,
A friendlier cat you've never met,
She comes and goes through her flap,
But best of all she loves my lap.

June Brown

SHEP

Brown white and sable
With almond eyes able
To show his every thought
Bushy tail wagging white chest bragging
To be your companion aught
Man's best friend it seems
Has always the means
To show just how he feels
Curse him, misuse him even abuse him
And when your temper has died
Whistle a call that he knows
And his loyalty grows
He'll lay down content by your side
Affectionate, loving in every way
But I didn't find him, he found me,
When he came to my house as a stray!

Jeff Jones

To Bruno - A Faithful Friend

I've just come into an empty house, no welcome bark,
No tail thumping against a door, no nose snuffling in my bags,
You have gone - never to return,
From fluffy pup, to faithful friend, we watched you grow, a guardian
Warning strangers - a friend to those you know.
Your head turning from side to side when we spoke to you, your soft
Brown eyes saying, 'I try to understand.'
Children on their way to school, petting you, as you stand so patient
Waiting for your walk.
The end so sudden, your eyes pleading, saying 'I'm sorry' the final
Gesture of a true and loving friend, there will never be another like you.
I look at your picture and remember happy days, a paw placed on my
knee saying 'Come and play' or 'Feed me!'
Teasing us with your toys, growling, trying to be fierce. Dear, gentle
Bruno, no pet will ever take your place.
As I write, no rhymes or verse, just a tribute, my eyes fill with tears,
I say 'Goodbye old pal, you will always be in our hearts and memories,
You will always be our very special friend.'

Eileen Hoyle

UNTITLED

What would I do without you,
You're always there for me,
Who else could I confide in,
Who else drinks my milky tea?

You do as you're told
Without any fuss
If it's jumping off a cliff
Or running under a bus.

As soon as I call you
You're instantly there,
Wagging your tail back and forth
Those big eyes a stare.

When I wake up in the morning
And look across the bed
He's all snuggled up like a puppy
My four-year old dog named Ted.

As soon as I go down the stairs
He's only two steps behind me
Then out he goes for a look around
And back in for his cuppa tea.

Now it's time for his doggy chew
And I will have some toast
He waits beside me for all the crusts
That's the bit he likes the most!

Next it's time to play with his favourite toy
He throws it around and shakes it
He really is full of joy!

A G Trick

GILBERT

Gilbert was my cockerel friend
Who drove our neighbours around the bend
For his cock-a-doodle sound
Could be heard for miles around.
For hours we would play
Each and every day
Gilbert even knew his name
Because he was so very tame
But sadly my poor Gilbert died.
Oh how I cried and cried
But I don't think my dad was sad
Because he said something really bad.
At dinner time one Sunday
There was chicken on our plates
I can't believe what Dad said
There's good this Gilbert tastes
Although my dad was lying
He couldn't stop me crying.
How could my dad forget
That poor old Gilbert was my pet.

Marie Horridge

GOODBYE BEN

I once had a friend, so faithful and true
But I lost him one day, right out of the blue,
He never complained when he was unwell.
He acted so normal that I barely could tell.
But the vet was called and the news was grim
And I hardly had time to say goodbye to him.
He died at home in my arms that dear friend,
As I was privileged to be with him at the end.
For weeks I cried, I was deep in despair
Then, one day in my garden I saw him there.
I know that he came, for I saw him so clear.
It was his way of showing me that he was near.
When my grieving ceased he stopped calling on me
Then I knew for certain that he was happy and free.
I haven't forgotten him; and I never will
For in my mind's eye, I can see him still
And one day I know we'll be together again
Me and my wonderful, darling Ben.

Lorraine Bosworth

ALLY MY BOY

I love you wee Ally
You were a gift to me.
You're precious in every way
My wee boy is quite a character in all ways.
He is named after a Scottish football player
Who I think is great,
Just like my wee Ally,
He loves the attention from one and all
He shouts 'Look at me, look at me,' I just
Want a pat from you all.
We all love and adore you,
You are there for us all,
So Ally this poem is for you *my wee boy*
Just to say thank you for coming to us.

Sharon Smith

BARNEY, MY DOG

He is my great protector,
He is my special friend.

A very special someone
On whom I can depend.
When strangers come a calling
At any time of day or night
He is a great alarm,
He's the one with whom they'll fight.

He really is a gentle creature,
He is a silly one
A sloppy great big duffer
If ever I saw one.
He will climb upon the bed
When he thinks I cannot see
At night when I am lonely
He rests his head upon my knee.

When the postman is around
He will know some time before,
Those most unwanted bills
Come dropping through the door.
He thinks he is the boss
That he is a great breadwinner
He will mooch around the house
Until he gets his dinner.

After all he's just a dog
Who wants taking for a walk.
A bit of warm affection
But!
I wish that he could talk.

Still he's my baby, he's intelligent,
He's clever, he's not dim.

Brenda Nicolson

PETS TODAY, PETS TOMORROW

I have seen people transformed
Thru the love of a dog,
I've seen strong men cry
Thru the loss of a dog
I am at a loss for words
Thru the love
And the loss
Of a dog.

Jenny Cupac

BONNIE

(In memory of Bonnie - Yorkshire Terrier who died aged 13 - 1993)

You made me happy
You comforted me when I was sad
I'll never find another friend like you
You're the best I've ever had.

You made me laugh
You made me cry
The worst day of my life
Was the day that you died.

I will never forget
My four-legged friend
You were loyal and faithful
Right to the end.

The illness you had
Made you go blind
Another good friend like you
Will be very hard to find.

I'll never forget you Bonnie
You were the best
But God knew you were old
And he took you to rest.

It's been seven lonely years
Since you passed away
Goodbye little girl
I miss you every day.

Well thank you my friend
For giving me so much love
The bright star at night
Lets me know you're above.

Shelley Edwards

DAVID THE DRAGON

I have a pet dragon who lives under my bed,
With sharp pointed teeth and eyes glowing red.
He tries to breathe fire but can only manage smoke,
I laugh and laugh and laugh, but he doesn't like the joke.
My mum tells me 'Don't be silly dragons don't exist,'
But there's something under my bed I think she might have missed
For *David* is real, as real as you and me.
And if you look under my bed *David* you shall see,
He does not eat, he does not drink, he does not even speak.
Instead he spends most of the time curled up asleep.
If you don't believe me I don't so much care,
Because I know *David the Dragon* is really there.

Charlotte Jeffery (12)

SILKY, MY BEST FRIEND

Silky is my guinea pig
But also my best friend.
She's not like any other pal,
She's original, she's unique.
She's warm and happy,
Her fur is black, ginger and white
And the most silky that I've ever seen.
Her eyes are deep, deep black.
She's a lovely guinea pig,
She can take food from your hand.
Friendly and warm natured,
That's Silky by the book!

Joanne Thomas (11)

A SORROWFUL DAY

Sometime ago a black feline cat came to our door.
She looked unwanted, her eyes said 'Oh, please take me in.'

We chose to call her *Blackie* she brought us lots of joy.

Alas, at 15 years she passed away. It was very upsetting.
Her strength was ebbing when pneumonia set in. She was
Too weak to resist.

Her closing eyes said 'Please don't replace me I loved you
Both so much.'

What sensitivity, she will remain in our hearts forever.
Without doubt she enhanced our life for good.

J F Jenkins

MY DOG - BILLY

You're one in a million,
You're special to me,
Affectionate, loyal
And good company.
You're there when I'm lonely
And life seems a bore,
You cheer me and offer
A comforting paw.
The look in your eyes
Says you quite understand
As you thrust a bewhiskered
Wet nose in my hand,
You never desert me,
Wherever I go,
You're a far better friend.
Than some people I know,
This short monologue
Is to my faithful, devoted
Companion - my dog.

Cynthia Hall

WHISKEY WAGGY TAIL

Little Whiskey Waggy Tail
Lives in Abbey Park
When you knock on our front door
You're bound to hear her bark.

She charges round and round the room
Like someone gone insane
It's up the stairs and down the stairs
Her bark would numb your brain.

You shout, in vain, to shut her up
And just increase the noise
You fight to drag her from the door
You trip across her toys.

The visitor outside, of course
Has heard this fearful din
And naturally considers on
The beast which lurks within.

He feels his palms go sweaty
His knees begin to knock
He just decides to leg it
When he hears the door unlock.

The door then slowly opens
He feels his heart must fail
Then trotting up to lick his hand
Is Whiskey Waggy Tail!

Hugh McIlveen

THE DOGS' HOME

Round and round the run they ran with tails all wagging high,
Abandoned, beaten, lost and scorned, enough to make you cry.
Little ones with lopped off tails, and dogs with shabby fur
Cross-breeds, mongrels, well-bred breeds, a hound dog type of cur.
One sits alone and takes no part in the mad excited dance
As if he knows, deep down inside, he hasn't got a chance,
He's had so many owners who never took the time
To try to understand him, and now he's past his prime.
He sits and broods and wonders how, with his sad life near spent
A happy, joyful lively pup could become this malcontent,
So leave him there, alone and sad, ignore him if you can
Just one more victim of the crude inhumanity of man.

Mair Patchett

PLEASE, NO MORE TEARS!

I'm looking down on you now
And would just like to say
'Please, no more tears,'
You made my pain go away.

You did much more for me,
Than most owners would
And would have paid anything
To make me better if you could.

But being a spaniel
With long golden hair,
My genes were contaminated
The illness was always there.

Then eventually one day,
I felt I couldn't go on,
So you called on a vet,
Who said to help me along.

I'm now in a place,
I'm happy at last.
But I will never ever
Forget all my past.

You meant so much to me,
As I did to you,
But I do understand
In the end, what else could you do?

A Williams

SPUD

You were just so fragile, a tiny ball of white,
You captured my heart - at the very first sight
You'd fit in my palm - with some room to spare,
Little red eyes, gave a little lost stare,
Bewildered she hid - in her own tiny house
What is it? Someone asked, is it a mouse?
Why, no - she's a hamster, let's give her a name
She's scared at the moment, no one's to blame.
She probably misses her mum, she's lost and confused,
Oh look, she's hidden, in Gemma's new shoes,
We must look after her properly - lots of tenderly care,
To feed her and love her, a responsibility we share.
I'm sure she will give us, lots of love in return,
With her funny tricks, that we will help her to learn.
We're talking of you Spud, you gave us such pleasure
Four years of loving memories - that we can now treasure
You loved your wheel, you'd go round and round
You'd roll in your ball all over the ground,
You knew when I called you - you'd come over to see
And you'd look, as to say - 'Have you something for me?'
Ginger biscuits were a favourite - you'd munch away
You liked lettuce and apple and cheese every day.
You were cheeky and mischievous - my dear little friend
The pleasures you brought us - never seemed to end.
A few months before Christmas, you grew very lame,
You didn't play so much, old age was to blame,
Towards the end of your life - you seemed to go blind
You weren't able to play - it seemed so unkind.
I was with you at the end Spud when you slipped away
God bless you fluffy little Spud - you're still thought of each day.

Janet Kelly

In The Beginning

Cleo, we had you for years and years and years
So naturally we shed a few tears
When finally you passed on
For you were the first one
In a long line of feline friends
You taught us how to love
God's little creatures from above
You brought a spark of light
Which began to glow so bright
And you brought kittens too
Which grew and grew and grew
Then came Marmaduke
An inspiration for any book
He wandered in as a stray
And eventually decided to stay
We didn't mind at all
But then Cleo began to call
Before we knew it was her need
There were other mouths to feed
We didn't realise just how fast cats breed
So with care in mind take heed
If you love your kitten dear
Don't wait until a litter or two appear.
For homes are hard to find these days
There are far too many strays
You will find it always pays
To see the vet right away
For it is better not to delay
So think; then spey.

Joan King

DUSTY

Dusty is a little dog
Now, Dusty isn't small,
He cocked up his little leg
And weed against the wall.

He saw the wall was smoking
He thought it was on fire.
So he cocked up his little leg
And weed a little higher.

Mary Brown

IN MEMORY OF YASMIN

She was loved.
By football-playing little boys
For always being full of the joys
Of Spring.
By local cricketers preparing for their game
For always coming when her name
Was called.
By the cats she lived with, but never chased
Spit, Polish, Thomas and Jethro,
Never threatened, but graced
By her presence.
By Arnold, closest friend and fellow Shar-Pei,
By Magic, who arrived last year and showed her how to play
Those puppy games again.
By the Staffie on the corner who thought she was a dear
And followed her through daffodils, although she made it clear
Her affections lay elsewhere.
In Heathlake Woods when going for a walk
By children, wanting to stop and talk
To the dog with the ever-wagging tail.
By family and friends and all who had the privilege to know
This brave and beautiful little dog, whose time to go
Came much too soon.
She was loved.

Linda Glew

MY DOG

Not many people can say they've a friend,
A close loving friendship that never will end
Someone to cuddle when you feel things are bad
To constantly comfort you when you feel sad.
They give love without question and don't ask for much.
Just a walk and some food and your loving touch.
Whenever you need them they nuzzle up close
Always right there when you need them the most
Never again will you find a friend like a dog
Who is faithful and sincere to the end.

Jane Carter

THE TOO COOL CAT

The cat was locked out, but more was put out, with
No one about, her tea was in doubt
She started to shout, the boiler was out, its flame not alight,
The house cold as night
She cowered in fright, at her helpless plight, no comfort in sight,
In this winters night.
She pawed at the floor, she pawed at the door, she pawed at thin air,
Her throat was so sore.
The noise of the car, her jaw wide ajar, her tail stretching far,
To show pleased we are!
The rubbing cat's touch, a trifle too much, delaying the opening
Of the human hutch.
The key in the door, the greatest of sounds, her human once lost,
Now happily found
The chink on her plate, a nice piece of skate, or liver or rabbit,
She longingly ate.
Her appetite quashed, her whiskers are washed, her ears as before,
With her wetted claw.
She licks every part, her tongue like a dart, covers her mane,
In the state of the art
She retires to the pipes that send heat through the floor, she snuggles,
She curls, en-hungered no more.
If humans will not, let sleeping dogs lie, she mews in disgust,
At her blighted shut eye.
For now she's forgotten her subservience, her life is her own,
Her pleasure intense
The *Do Not Disturb* sign in much evidence.

T J Brumby

My Dog's Name Is Jinx

My dog's name is *Jinx*
Phew, she stinks
With big brown eyes
A little button nose
So full of mischief
Wherever she goes
She's shaped like a bubble
And always in trouble
She picks on her brother
But never no other.
You chew the slugs
And pounce on the bugs
You dive at my daughter
And bent her nose
Run in the garden
And bring back a rose

Bathtimes I dread
Before you lay down your sleepy head.
So up to the tub
To give you a scrub
 I turn on the taps
And move out the mats
She snarls and growls,
Plays tug-of-war with the towels
And there's more water over me than she.
I look a wreck
The bathroom's in a worse state than me,
But she's my loveable rogue you see.

Gloria Whitehouse

CASPER THE CROSS-BRED HOUND

Why I should love you I really don't know
Except that I've cared for you and watched you grow
From a cute little puppy with crinkly face
To a large hairy dog that takes up too much space.

You're silly, destructive and bark all the time
And sometimes I try to pretend you're not mine
You dig up the garden to bury your bone
And howl if you hear a police car or phone.

The children adore you, they laugh when you're rude
Then you knock them all down and inspect them for food
You really are useless, a guard dog you're not
You're scared of the postman, the milkman, the lot.

You just want to play with a toy or a ball
And mostly ignore the commands that I call
I can't get it into your daft doggy head
That you sleep in the kitchen and not on the bed.

You think you are human and we are your pack
We do all the work while you lie on your back
If not carefully cosseted day after day
You sulk like a baby that can't have its way.

With those big liquid eyes and that slobbery tongue
You don't understand your behaviour is wrong
I love you and yet as you sleep on your rugs
I can't help but wish that you wouldn't eat slugs.

Christine Crook

THE HAMSTERS' LOT

Take a peek, the hamsters' wheel goes squeak, squeak, squeak,
They run but get nowhere, the phone rang the other day,
It was my daughter's friend, her pet hamster had gone to Hamster,
Heaven, she sobs as her prize pet is laid to rest, a plot in the garden,
In the shade by the shed is thought best. Hamsters live for a year,
Or two at the most, the parents decide to buy another.
It is an answer to the little girl's plight, but, these creatures are
Nocturnal, they are awake all night, they gnaw at the cage.
To try to escape, ours got into next door, they were in a rage.
If I am right, the hamsters must live on their own, or they
Will fight, the male when he has mated must be taken away
For he will kill the litter, the bald and the blind, don't they
Know their own kind? What a futile, boring short life,
Still they give pleasure to the owners for a little short while.
The goldfish all die, they don't live long, the budgie died in
The cold, if they don't live for long then they shouldn't be sold.
I will not now, have any more pets, when they go, we only
Get upset, we had a Yorkshire Terrier for seventeen
Glorious years, he was a good friend, he came everywhere
With me but for his own good we had to have him put down
In the end but still, whatever I say, at the end of the day
Hamsters will still be the same, they seem to possess a zest
For their very short quest, so have a hamster if you may
I don't know how much you will have to pay, but remember
They live two years at the most.

Richard Shurey

ABEL

Abel is a red and white boxer,
Some say, a human with four legs
And whenever he wants to be noticed
He barks, he yelps and he begs.

Although five years old, he's a baby
Give him a ball and he's your best friend
He'll run, jump and play like a puppy
But if a stranger appears, he'll defend.

Abel is a big part of our family
He has his own bed and a big box of toys
He likes stones, balls, rattles and chews
But it's our bed that he really enjoys.

When he sleeps, he goes into a coma
Lying on his back with his legs in the air
With mouth open he always starts snoring
But with cotton wool in our ears, we don't care.

Some people say that Abel is ugly
With squashed face and big droopy eyes
And some have even called him a slaver
But with a mouth like his, that's no surprise.

We do our best to look after Abel
And know we don't treat him like a dog
Sometimes strict, but we always reward him
Knowing he will always be there as our guard.

The boxer will be a good friend and companion
Always walking proud and true on their lead
Let them know that you care and protect them
And they will obey your every need.

Brian John Green

KITTEN IN THE MARIGOLDS

Kitten in the marigolds
hiding, watching,
Kitten in the marigolds
watching me.
Kitten in the marigolds
thinks he's hidden,
Kitten in the marigolds
I can see.

Kitten in the marigolds
slowly creeping,
Kitten in the marigolds
drawing near,
Kitten in the marigolds
quietly crouching,
Kitten in the marigolds
feels no fear.

Kitten in the marigolds
practising hunting,
Kitten in the marigolds
stalking flies.
Kitten in the marigolds
feeling weary,
Kitten in the marigolds
sleeping lies!

H Lobo

BONNIE

Rambling through the hills
clad in purple heather behind my house.
Bonnie, my border collie
never chased sheep or even grouse.
She was a companion closer than a friend.

Her span of time was brief,
a mere ten years of life.
She filled my soul with joy
relieving me of worldly strife.

Walking on the hills alone now,
I wander down memory lane.
I miss my four-legged friend of yesteryears
and unashamedly shed a few tears.

Engaged in thoughts of bygone days
of my obedient, faithful, playful friend.
Shall I forget that sad farewell -
A friendship torn apart, by your sudden end.

J Henderson Lightbody

A Dog's Life
(In memory of our little dog, Susie Cue)

I wake up every morning, to be let out for a wee,
Come back in time for breakfast, a dog chew, drink of tea,
Then I'm taken for a walk, just around the park
Often meet another breed, give a sniff, then a bark.
Not long before we're home again, my boss how soon he tires,
There you'll find me dreaming full-stretch before the fire,
Later on another run, back in time for dinner
I'm a good dog if I eat it up, if not, I'm called a sinner!
I usually manage most of it, 'cause then I get a treat
I sit up, for 3 chocolate drops, they're what I'd call my sweet,
I often pay a visit to my friends' just two doors up
They've always made me welcome ever since I was a pup.
It's nice to have an extra pat, a rub behind the ear
And know they're there to run to and they live so very near.
So that's a dog's life it is, well I'm glad I fit the bill,
I don't have any work to do and always get my fill,
But all dog's aren't so lucky, some struggle to get by,
So when I'm told to *be a good boy*, really I do try!

Eve Mackuin

ROCKY

Rocky was a great wee dog
But now he's gone to stay with God
For the time we had him was such a pleasure
Our memories we will always treasure.
He was so bright and so clever
Almost as if he could talk
Just one look from him seemed to say
'Please can I go for a walk?'
Peter and Veronica they had him, they were so glad
So sad now he has gone away
But up above watching you day by day
His tail waging and his lips a-licking
Having his favourite - a plate of chicken
We all will miss him up at the club
Even when we're having a nice wee jug
And from time to time while having a drink
Of wee Rocky Boo we will always think.

Peter Miller

MY LADY

A little story, I want to tell
about a dear friend and pal of mine
who I got to know quite well.
My pal, she was a border collie
which tells us quite a lot
I gave her the name *Lady*
now what a wonderful *Lady* I've got.
We would play, go for walks
over fields and the like
many a mile we would tread
then we'd head back home.
Have our meal, then later, off to bed.
The years went by so quickly
for both *Lady* and for me.
We were inseparable, happy as can be.
Then, alas, one day, my *Lady* she became unwell.
A sadness I felt inside.
She looked so peaceful
and yet, seemed so happy, then my poor *Lady* died.

M W Kell

SUKI AND THE LAMB

Late Spring
an elderly Siamese cat
greatly loved
went for a walk with her human tribe
in a garden of Eden - like landscape
at Ickworth Park.

She walked well
through the long grass
and enjoyed
the early evening sunlight.

On resting, she jumped down
from the hurdle
and looked back,
beckoning to follow her.

On being carried
for fear she may have walked too far,
she insisted on going to the ground
and investigating a lamb
who was likewise interested in her.

Was this the lion laying down with the lamb,
was the Lord Jesus, the heavenly Lamb of God
preparing her for a transfer
from this life
to the Holy Mount of God?

Victor Weston

A SHAGGY DOG STORY

The best day of my young life and face to face,
I could see eyes inquisitive yet full of grace.
A nuzzle from a cold wet nose,
As if to say I am here, and yes hello.
With a collar made of red velvet ribbon,
He was to me on my twelfth birthday given.
Such a cute bundle of fluff with big floppy ears,
My wish at last granted it moved me to tears.
He trusted people, only God knows why,
Eight weeks old found abandoned, left to die.
His coat smoky grey, soft and silky,
Parentage unknown maybe black Poodle and Yorkie.
A sweet and loving nature he obviously possessed,
To everyone that met him so generously expressed.
First day he found a fledgling and ran indoors for help,
Stirring deep emotion of his own beginnings no doubt.
After all his suffering, trouble and strife,
We both together began a new and richer life.

S Gillian Forth

OUR ANIMALS' PEOPLE

If people were animals
And animals people,
Where would we then be?

Would we constrain them,
Cajole them,
Castrate and inject them,
Then cook them up for our tea?

Would we shoot them, and cage them,
Brand them and scar them,
Debeak and entrap them,
Then charge consumers the fee?

. . . or would we be kind?

Colin Davies

MY DOG

One very cold December night, I spotted such a special sight.
For there in my garden, looking ever so sweet,
Was the cutest little dog, you ever could meet,
I guessed she'd been abandoned, but I'll never really know,
And one thing I was certain, she didn't want to go.
Without delay, I opened my door,
Her sad little plight, I just couldn't ignore,
Two plates of food, were gulped down in haste,
She barely had time, to savour the taste.
Licking her lips, she quickly made way,
To the fireside rug, on which she then lay.
She curled herself round, in a cute little heap,
Then in no time at all, she had fallen asleep.
The police were informed, in case she had strayed,
But despite all their efforts, no claim was ever made,
So *Flossie* as I've called her, now spends her days with me,
And a far nicer doggie, there never could be,
She does some quite amazing tricks,
She chases balls and fetches sticks,
To get my attention, she'll offer her paw,
Her cute pleading eyes, I just cannot ignore.
At night she sneaks up to my bed,
She has her own, but likes mine instead.
I take her to the park each day, she loves to run around and play,
She follows me about, from morning till night,
Wagging her tail, with constant delight,
And when I sit down, she climbs on my lap,
Curls up in a ball and takes a quick nap.
She may be just a dog, but she's also my best friend,
'Cause on her total loyalty, I know I'll always depend.

Susan Boulter

EMOTIONAL CANINE

Kayden is a full size German Shepherd
He has tracked across the world,
Spent months in quarantine like a leopard,
He lost his master overseas
But returned to England with high fees.

He had to settle in his new home
But because he barked people would moan
When in his Australian home he would roam
But now he's in the country of the Millennium Dome.
It took him a long time to settle
One vet announced *Put him down.*

At this prospect everyone frowned
We knew he had to have a chance
He's a big softy, but large at a glance,
Another vet said 'He was going blind,'
He's proved them wrong, he's now fine.

He looks after his Master's wife,
He notifies her if there's any strife
He's the best guard dog for miles around
Now he's settled down, no one murmurs a sound.
He may make one's legs a'wobble
And if he jumped up, he would make you topple.

He loves to jump and play
He'll dance with your feet and lick you all day.
If anyone dares enter near,
Then Neighbourhood Watch hears him clear,
But under the loud noise of his bark
Is a puppy so tender and so smart.

Sheralee Le-Gros

BOOMER

(A faithful companion for almost 16 years, died peacefully 13/12/1996. Missed by all his friends)

I put my hand down by my chair
Then I remember you're not there
I didn't want to let you go
But couldn't see you suffer so
I held you close my faithful friend
As your life with dignity did end.

Sometimes when I'm feeling sad
I think of the happy times we had
Of how you loved to romp and play
A pal to all whom came your way
At the world you wagged your tail
Then slowly your health began to fail.

The sad day came when we had to part
Though you're gone from our lives
You remain in our hearts.

B Leigh

FAMILY PET

Hare and tortoise was it a fable?
He did win, because he was able.
Don't be misled, they're not so slow,
Good food, sunlight and away they go.
Fun in sun, or run in the rain,
Our Speedy could win an Olympic game.
He's smart, clever, but needs a mate,
Tried our Cilla - for blind date.
He's now 2 score years and one,
In his prime and looking for fun,
Speedy Gonzarliz is his name,
Early 60's music, got him his fame.
The pleasure he's given to big and small,
He wobbles, limps and even slight fall,
Tea in morning, and on a plate.
Bangs the door, if it arrives late.
What's going to happen when we are gone!
Would he last with someone new this long?
We'll leave him with someone who'll give him love,
So, we can look down on him, from up above.

Sheila Donetta

PLEASE TAKE ME HOME

I am quite old with just one eye
But I can still see all the people walk by
I sit in a tiny cage with just a small run
Day after day not much fun.

What is it like to sit on someone's knee,
Take me home, take care of me.

Please pick me up and give me a cuddle
Trust me I will be no trouble.

Jenny Plant

WHAT'S THE POINT?

You feed 'em, you water 'em,
You groom 'em, you walk 'em,
You bath 'em, you bed 'em,
Then they go and die on you.
What's the point of having a dog?

In the photo album, what do I see?
Worshipping eyes looking out at me.
Then I remember ears so floppy,
A canine kiss, ever so sloppy.
What's the point of having a dog?

The upraised paw, eyes that plead,
Wagging tail as I pick up the lead.
From lolling tongue saliva drips,
Expectant eyes, and licking lips.
What's the point of having a dog?

Once more I hear the joyful bark,
As I throw the ball in the local park.
With a dog of your own
You are never alone!
That's the point of having a dog?

J P Manghan

MY CATS

My cats are called Snowy and Misty.

One has brown fur, one has white,
They hiss at each other and give us a fright,
Both of them were homeless and
Had nowhere to go at night,
Now in their beds they sleep in delight.
They're beautiful and loving that's what I think,
A saucer of warm milk that's what they
Like to drink.
They sleep in their beds, at night just like us,
They moan and miaow and make a fuss,
They play in the garden, it's great to see,
I throw a piece of scrunched up paper,
They play with me
But I love them and they love me,
It makes me happy,
That they're in my family.

Leanne Bridgewater (10)

A TRIBUTE TO EBONY

A tribute to someone special, Ebony was his name,
He belonged to my Lisa but part of the family he became.
Ebony in colour, Ebony by name, they looked the
Perfect picture as she rode him down the lane.
She straight in the saddle, with him his head held
High, a sight to be noticed as they walked by.
Many shows were entered, rosettes were won
I think what mattered more was just to have fun.
To canter round the fields with the wind in their hair,
You only had to watch them to see the love that was there,
Alas it could not last for long, so poorly he became
His legs were affected so he became lame.
Lisa had a decision to make, which cost her very dear,
I can guess it wasn't made without many a tear.
But they were both very lucky, if they can think of
It like that
Those few happy years together which no one can take back
And she can still ride him in her dreams down the pony track
So my lovely Lisa remember each day like new
You loved him oh so much, but he did you too!

Doreen Biddiscombe

A FRIEND AND GOOD COMPANION

As she lay her head upon my lap
and gazed into my eyes
I remember those years of happiness we had
a friend and good companion.
Those long walks in the countryside
lonely nights when you stayed by my side
fun and laughter in the garden
those baths you never liked
that last look at me as you closed your eyes
tears fell from my eyes
a friend and good companion.
The door opened quietly
she has gone now, I will take her away
stay a while said the vet
for it's hard to lose a dog you love
a friend and good companion.

Trevor Watmuff

FRIENDS

You greet me with
Great bounds of joy
Of open true affection
You do not lie
You do not cheat
You do not know deception
You are my protectors
I am yours
You are my dogs
I love you, my friends.

P Beal

FINAL SLUMBER

Dead of night and the streets are void,
silence prevails, all is tranquil and still.
The cat with a mouse he has toyed,
roams around his territory proudly after his kill.

He darts across the road with such elegance,
powerful muscles quickly flex his agile legs.
Leaping with such grace over a wooden fence,
locates his favourite spot amongst the flower beds.

His coat marked with black and ginger patches,
appears as a mask around eyes of green.
Stretching upwards, upon a wooden post he scratches,
emphasising to other cats where he has been.

He licks and grooms his long glossy fur,
amongst the flowers in the sultry night.
Sniffing the sweet aroma of the fragrant air,
then slumbers peacefully till the morning light.

He emerges, stretching lazily from his scented bed,
standing high on his legs with his back curved.
Suddenly he's struck on the side of his head,
by a speeding car that never swerved.

Lying in the gutter ignored from passers by,
I picked him up and home I carried.
With a saddened heart and a tearful eye,
a forgotten cat that morning I buried.

Embraced in a scrap of old velvet curtain,
like a foetus curling under from its head.
This poor little cat was dead for certain,
I scuffed dust over a patch of red.

Martin Howard

MY FRIEND SASHA

My neighbour's cat's so clever
He lives across the way.
A silent miaow through the window
And he visits me each day.
Out of the upstairs bedroom window
Onto a canopy above the door
Then he saunters down the wall
And dashes across to my door.
He lies upon my knees and his head
I gently pat.
Thank you for the love he purrs.
My gorgeous pussy cat.

B Walker

SIMPLY THE BEST

I like cats me,
I think cats are cool.
Cats can be so laid back
That's why they're nobody's fool,
Cats are their own soul,
They tolerate the rest
To put it simply, cats
Are the best.

Peter de Dee

TENDER

Curl beside me,
beautiful cat.
place your paw
on my cheek
and we'll both
take a nap.
As breathing deepens,
to a regular beat,
your purring,
gently
aids my sleep.

Amy Phillips

TOMMY 1ST

Frightened little one-eyed puss
Came one day to stay with us
Not so very sure was he
That this was where he should be

He came and went for quite awhile
Then he settled down in style
His eye was better and he could see
How very much he meant to me

For five long years his life was good
Full of warmth and love and food
Then God took him, in his way
Ever more with him to stay

Susanne Humphries

POSH KAT (SIR BLACKIE)

Once a small, cute, black kitten
He came from a very large litter.
Now a large, gigantic, panther-like thing,
Who sounds like a record stuck,
When he begins to sing.

As he tip-toes around on his soft, silky feet,
And sits in the cool shade when he feels the heat.
Swings his long black, bushy tail,
And flutters his wide green eyes,
Reaching out with his sharp claws,
Trying to catch the fast flying flies.

He purrs like a buzzing bee
Miaows loudly and acts like a she, instead of being a he.
Sleeps and dreams of a dish of milk and meat,
Love and adventure to make his day complete.

Living in first class, no need to run fast,
Yet stalk and leap behind the settee.
To feel at peace - yet to be tricked out
By a crunchy treat . . .

His eyes are lit to the sights of stairs,
A trio of rooms - unknown what he may get up to.
Yet he runs up them as if
His tail were as springy as Tigger's hopping lift.
That once-playful cat still exists.
As tender his voice he miaows,
A sloppy kiss is to be found.
Because as soon at that magic word 'meat' can be said
He with his tail high, goes triumphantly back down.

Ann Worrell

JACKEY

The hillside was bleak and grim.
Black clouds crowded overhead.
A bitter wind blew strongly
And sleet began to fall.

Jackey sensed something was wrong -
His master seemed slow and plodding today,
Checking for early lambs
Against the great expanse of the mountain.

The wind moaned on,
Tearing at the man's jacket, and Jackey's fur.
His eyes were keen and troubled,
Watching his master falter.

Snow started falling rapidly -
Visibility reduced to a pace or two.
The man's breathing was faster,
Gasping, always gasping - fighting for air.

Jackey stayed close,
His whimpering lost in the roar of the wind.
Darkness was falling rapidly -
Darkness came suddenly to the man.

He fell heavily,
Dropping like a sack of black, dirty coal.
Jackey, urged him up,
His wet nose pushing so gently at his master's face.

It was light before they were found.
Man dead. Jackey barely alive.
Two small boulders against the mountain's vastness -
The freezing snow claiming victory.

S Wood

WHAT A CHARLIE!
(In beloved memory of 'Charlie' - died March 2000, aged 14)

Our lovely pussy cat with beige fur,
We wake in the mornings to hear you purr.
At the foot of the bed we hear you move,
We pat your head, so warm and smooth.

The postman arrives and delivers the mail,
You charge downstairs with a flick of your tail,
Purring to get your breakfast underway,
Cornflakes and toast first, it's just not your day!

To bed we go at the end of the day,
Letting you in later when you have your say,
Sometimes it is just hard to comprehend -
A cat who was more than just a friend.

You sat and listened to our every word,
We talked to you - no, it's not absurd!
But now Charlie Boy, you can finally rest,
Sleep well faithful friend, and God bless.

B J Wood

DARLING CATS

She would peep around the curtain to surprise me,
Then jump right up and cuddle on my lap,
White as snow with spots of cinnamon and slate,
So loving was my darling Asbury cat.

With his strong, proud physique he'd roam the garden.
In his dreams he snored so loud upon the mat,
Silver shone upon his cloud-white chunky body,
So devoted was my darling Pee-Wee cat.

Such a little one, so tiny when he came here,
The television was his joy and his delight,
He plod slowly did my black-eyed little sweetheart,
So intelligent was darling Smarti cat.

She cries and moans and always wants attention,
Yet never shows her claws or tries to fight,
A fluffy little one, a stripy tiger,
So gentle is my darling girl Jem cat.

Donna Llewellyn-Kear

OUR PET

We had her when she was so small
Her head peeping out from a loving arm
A fuss of her was made by all
We talked to her to keep her calm.

Next we taught her right from wrong
Which took much longer than I thought
But never mind, it wasn't long!
We knew a lovely dog we'd bought.

Though she is not a pedigree
Alsatian/Greyhound cross you know
She runs like the wind you see
Just stand back and watch her go.

We have of course the chewing up
Of the odd slipper, wood and such
But after all, she's just a pup
And we all love her very much.

Sally, our puppy, full of fun
Keeps us fit with exercise
In the park she loves to run
Then panting on her bed she lies.

It is great to own a pet
Who's there for you when you come home
You'll have a kiss that's nice and wet
You know you'll never be alone.

Y Corcoran

OUR PUPPY - SPIKE'S SON

Our puppy is a little chap who may keep us awake at night,
He is a very cheeky soul who chews everything in sight.
While he is young he needs four meals every day
And in between sleeping he frequently wants to play.
At first he used to make little puddles on the floor,
Toilet training can be a very demanding chore!
Then suddenly the light dawns and he asks to go outside,
I pet him and praise him and reward him with pride.
When he plays in the garden we're frightened he may roam,
Then suddenly up he pops behind a garden gnome!
Running along the daffodils, biting off their heads,
Getting up to mischief in the flower-beds.
Sometimes I wonder if we've done the right thing,
Then I try to remember all the pleasure he will bring.
He looks at me and licks me and wags his little tail
And I know that to love him we simply cannot fail.
I know that we will love him more with every passing day,
And I know that he will love us too, come what may!

Christine Naylor

PRINCE CHARMING

Prince, my pet, my poodle so dear
A present for Christmas, he changed my life
This little black, woolly ball of fluff
Mischievous from waking up, to settling on my bed for the night
A constant companion, faithful and loving
He asks only for food, but gives much in return
When I am sad, he seems to know
He jumps on my lap and asks in his own little way for attention
I stroke his fur and give him a cuddle
Soon my mood changes for the better, sensing it
He jumps off my lap and looks at me, his tail wagging
He wants to play now his mission is accomplished
Legs prancing like a tap dancer he backs off, egging me on
At his level we roll about, before he charges off to fetch his toy
No longer am I sad, Prince has worked his charm
He is almost thirteen now, sadly I wonder how much time he has left
Before he has to leave, forever
He doesn't see as well now, his hearing is deteriorating, his
joints stiffening
But still he is happy, still full of fun, still a puppy at heart,
As he was that very first Christmas
He is my companion and friend
He will always be mine right up to the end.

Kerry Metcalfe

UNTITLED

My master threw me out today
After five, long loving years
Then I'm only a dog you know!
My heart is broken I've lost my best friend.
I'm only a dog you know!
Waiting in my new home
Hoping my old master will call
Then I'm only a dog you know!
How sad it is when you can't ask why,
I can't say I love them
So then I'm only a dog you know!
How could they do this to me
After five loving years with them
Then I'm only a dog you know!

R E Torn

PIPPIN

December	A little poodle as black as could be, was born but was unknown to me.
January	We met, all black and curly, a wonderful pet, full of life just like a bubble, did he mean a lot of trouble?
February	He's all wobbly and just looks like a little black lamb, Am I going to love him, I'm sure I am.
March	We bought him a lead and collar, tried to walk him but he wouldn't follow.
April	Pippin feels spring in the air and oh what fun he not only walks, he can run.
May	Pippin's behaviour is much the same, He's so fit and loves to play he *will* do as I ask, some day.
June	My birthday month, I treat him to a ball, Will he bring it back? Not at all!
July	He has his puppy trim, he seems to know He's as proud as a king.
August	I have got my own flat, Mum gave me a leaving present No not china, something finer - Pippin.
September	Paint and paper everywhere, My bathroom is yellow and so is my little fellow!
October	Very cold and frosty, leaves have fallen off the trees Pippin loves to smell at these.
November	Snowflakes falling all around, completely covering the ground. Pippin and myself have lots of fun, he's a lovely little boy.
December	A full year filled with love and fun, Pippin is now exactly one.

Phyllis Smith

BATTERSEA DOGS' HOME

Old Scruff was in his kennel
He tried to look his best
But he just couldn't compare
With any of the rest

Miss Dalmatian had the
Kennel across
The Collie Alsatian and
A Labrador called Josh

When people came to view
Old Scruff didn't get a glance
It was always the poodle or
The Great Dane called Hanse

Even though he looked real
Rough he had a heart of
Gold
And all the ones that pass
Him by they think that he's
Too old

But a better pet you couldn't
Find
For old Scruff was the best
One of a kind

Marilyn Davidson

FOR SAM

Dear Sam, you didn't deserve to die
In the manner that you did.
When you saw those bully-boys coming,
You should have run and hid.
But being such a friendly soul
They could grab you by the collar,
And squeeze the very life from you
So you couldn't even holler.
Then they hurled you down and broke you,
Not caring what they'd done,
They killed my loved, most precious, Sam
For a fleeting bit of fun.

Marilyn Locker

CAT TRAX

Little cat on the wall,
You do not make a noise at all.
Slender and sleek,
Across the garden tiptoe and sneak.
A black silhouette against the yellow moon,
Eyes as deep and green as a lagoon.
Soft paws make no sound,
On the damp dew-covered ground.
Through the cat flap up the stairs,
To her bed where she has no cares.
Till morning sleep my friend,
Until the night comes to an end!

Michelle Lee Landon (14)

THE COCKER SPANIEL

I was born with love of canine
Of anyone's dog, but especially mine.
I've always had complete affinity,
And no doubt will have until infinity.
But one breed stands out there all alone,
The *Cocker Spaniel* in a class of its own.

Being a somewhat visual person,
I appreciate shape, line, proportion,
And myriad variations of colour lie
Safely stored in my mind's eye.
The *Cocker Spaniel* has each of these
Qualities designed to please.

But all of this would count for nought
If he bit and snarled and fought.
Instead his friendly, joyful nature
As he twirls around in rapture,
Expressing unconditional love,
Makes one feel in Heaven above.

Ina J Harrington

BUNNYZONE

Each day, you bring such joy for me,
You make depression, disperse and flee.
Warm dark eyes and loppy ears,
A cuddle to allay all fears.
Little companions that trust me so much,
That bring such joy with a tender touch,
Few could understand the therapy you give,
A whole new reason, now to live.
A natural remedy, refreshing and strong,
My whole life changed when you came along.
A complete little family, unique stories to recount.
Every day, in the largest amount.
I thank the Lord for the joy each day,
Happiness, as I watch you play.
Contentment abounds, inspiration flows.
What is the magic? I just don't know.
Thumper Ponkin, Binker, Dee,
Bo Bo, Drewdy and William T.
Baby Angel, you all mean so much,
I am blessed by your healing touch.
May each day we share be richly blessed.
To bring such love and tenderness.

Janet Parry

KIRA

I remember the day I first brought you home,
A small lively puppy to call my own,
I picked you out from all the rest,
I must have known then you were the best.
Your petty face looked up at me,
Your big brown eyes looked pleadingly,
I looked after you like a mother,
We both learnt to trust one another.
I taught you lots of games and tricks,
Like begging, heeling, fetching sticks.
Thirteen years have quickly flown,
You're quite content to stay at home,
Walks must be kept short for your sake,
As arthritis makes your joints ache.
Although now, your pace is slow,
You're always happy and eager to go.
When visitors call, you don't want to know,
Under the table is where you go,
When I talk you listen patiently,
Tilting your head intermittently.
If I've been out I don't have to call,
I hear you pattering down the hall,
You welcome me with licks on the hand,
You always seem to understand.
At nine-thirty it's time for bed,
You lie on the pillow next to my head.
Over the years I've watched you grow,
You've helped me more than you'll ever know,
You are loyal and patient you are good company,
You've always been a friend to me.

Maura Walsh

LAMBERT (1984-1999)

He was there through teenage angst,
exams, marriage, please and thanks.

A face there by the open door,
everything, he joined and saw.

Running, springing, barking, wagging,
licking, chewing, chasing, dragging.

Walking the streets, enjoying the park,
with all he met, made his mark.

As years went by, age crept up,
yet somehow to us, remained a pup.

Times were, in rage we shouted,
but our love for him, never doubted.

Waiting alone in the car for us,
seeing us coming, always a fuss.

His mad ways, his protective bark,
towards the end, weak legs and heart.

Cared for then, through every hour,
sad to see him lose his power.

Funny, sweet, unique ways,
by our side he always stayed.

Fifteen years of memory,
our favourite dog he'll always be.

A family of three, he made four,
Sad September, with us no more.

Vanessa Ann Langford

PERKY-POLLY AND CRAZY CATS

I had a parrot who was very rude
And said lots of words that he never should.
One day he up and flew away
We never found him to this day.
But all the birds who live in our wood
Have put words to their songs which are very lewd.

I saw my cat fall off the roof
And that was absolutely proof
He'd been out on the tiles,
Of feline sport there'd been no lack,
For as he lay there on his back
His face was wreathed in smiles.

The very same cat was quite off his dot,
He just loved water, he loved it a lot.
Until one day he dived down the loo,
That cured his passion for water - pooh!

Two brother cats were sitting on the mat.
One of these cats spied a mouse which was fat.
That cat pounced swiftly and caught his prey,
And then proceeded with it to play.
He tossed the mouse high up in the air,
His brother cat caught it - it wasn't fair.
With the mouse in his mouth he ran away
Whilst the first cat, bewildered, searched all day.

Prudence M Jones

OUR GEORGE

Our George loves licking.
He's very good at licking.
He dreams about licking.
He picks as well.
He loves picking.
Probably more than licking.
In fact he does more picking than licking.
Our George loves licking.
Our George loves picking.

Our George studies people
To see if they lick and pick like he does.
He also watches dogs and wonders
why they don't lick and pick.
Or perhaps they do.
He hates the comb, in case
it stops him licking and picking.
Some say he's lousy. He's not lousy.
He just likes licking and picking.

Our George, the neighbours say,
Will die of licking and picking
or scoffing chicken.
He's mad about chicken.
He scoffs a lot of chicken.
He's good at scoffing chicken.
He's better at scoffing chicken
than licking and picking.
No! He's not a spoilt little brat.
Our George is a gorgeous ginger cat.

Maureen Walden

PENNY - THE JACK WITH ATTITUDE

Once we had a garden
Now it's just a mess.
Why the transformation?
You'll never ever guess.
She's a little dog called Penny
Who's sweet as sweet can be
She has the kindest nature
But does she love to pee!
Carpets, lino, flowers, grass
All are stained from Penny's ass.
She digs up all the flowers
In their places she plants bones.
I tell her 'Sit!' She jumps about
I tell her 'Stay!' I don't half shout.
Even though she's very naughty
I wouldn't want a pooch that's haughty.
Keep your classy ritzy dogs
They'd bore me near to tears
Penny is the one for me
Down from her tail up to her ears
She's lovely.

Anita Goddard

LOLLY'S PRAYER

I'm not the Archbishop nor the Pope in Rome,
I'm just a small cat that's found a new home,
They're very nice people I think you'll agree,
Two adults, two children and now there's me,
Dear Lord I know you're busy with this and that,
But please, God bless us all from Lolly the cat.

Harry Aspey

My Benjie

They found him tethered without food or drink
Unwanted, frightened and lost.
No collar, no name, an adult dog,
Discarded by people who can't count the cost.
Terrified of fireworks the thunder and rain,
He's now going deaf. Thank God!
He'll never be scared by noises again.

Nearly ten years ago I met my bundle of love
The kennel maids named him Scruffy
Nobody would take him home,
They much preferred a puppy.
They didn't notice his gorgeous eyes,
Which had softened the executioner's heart.
He was waiting. We bonded! Those eyes gazed at me.
My Benjie crept into *my* heart.

M R Newton

THE LOSS OF A PET (BENNY 1998)

I recently lost my pet,
To sleep he was put,
To be kind said the vet,
To end his life at fourteen,
He was only a teenager it seemed,
I am now eighty-one,
My pet has gone,
Each time I wander past trees,
Where he'd ponder,
I feel so depressed,
Was it for the best?
Now he is at rest,
In that kennel in the sky,
Will he be wondering why!
Will he meet his master when I die?
We will never know,
Where humans go,
God bless him though,
He meant so much to me,
Now I go walks where his spirit must be.

Ernest Cooper

MOGGY

Our little cat Moggy
Is a very fat Moggy
Who has a tum only
Two inches from the floor

She eats in the morning
And guards the food till night
Patti dare not go near
For fear there'll be a fight

She was given to us
When only two years old
Because she chased the birds
With havoc in the shop

Our little grey Moggy
Although a fat Moggy
Is a very sweet cat
And is loved at that

Joanne Spence

THE GOLDFISH

This one's all about a fish,
Swimming round a plastic dish,
He swims all day, he swims all night,
Does he sleep? I think he might!

I put a castle in his bowl,
I think he might prefer a goal,
But then he couldn't kick the ball,
He hasn't got much sense at all.

A lady fish might do the trick,
But then again he might be sick
Of bits and pieces in his tank,
I tried a ship but that just sank.

What about a change of food,
His blank look may be misconstrued,
It may be that he's getting old,
Perhaps he's caught a nasty cold.

There's not much left to tell you now,
The fish is dead I don't know how.
Perhaps the cold became the flu,
I'll have to flush him down the loo.

We're mourning for an empty bowl,
The children want to dig a hole,
To say a prayer to say goodbye,
He's in the glass bowl in the sky.

I'll have to get another pet,
I'll get a dog or better yet,
Perhaps a budgie or a cat,
Oh no I just don't fancy that!

I'll just say nowt then they'll forget,
About the poor departed pet,
Maybe they'll settle for a toy,
Yes that would be a better ploy.
I just can't stand the stress and strain,
Of pets that die, no not again!
The goldfish was the first and last,
We had to have the flag half-mast.

In future we will stick to games,
No more pets with silly names,
No more funerals, floods of tears,
We'll have him stuffed, he'll last for years!

Fyril Cletcher

ANIMAL HEAVEN

They say that horses and little foals and other animals have no souls.
I've heard otherwise quite intelligent people say so. How do
they know?
For to me it seems quite plain, if they'd only think again
That if we have souls then they have too, and if they've not,
no more we do.
To anyone who's made a friend of a cat or dog, or for that matter even a
hog: It must be clear, they're just like we are.
That is the trouble with Christianity, it seems to me to be over much
concerned with humanity.
We're told to believe just what we're taught, and just in case some
chance original thought drops into that void yawning wide and bursts
the bubble or our pride.
We must close the windows of our minds, pull down the blinds
Or we may stir up awkward questions and upset the whole scheme
of things, which is they say God's plan, for his masterpiece - *man.*
Now when I arrive at heaven's gate (will it be like some vast
celestial estate?)
Just supposing they're going to let me in, anyway (and it's doubtful if
they would) for I've not been particularly good
I'll say to St Peter 'Can my friends come in too, because without them
I simply cannot do?'
Will he jingle his keys and look benign, but shake his head and point
to the sign saying 'No dogs or cats, or rabbits or anything with
four-footed habits, no hares no hippopotamuses.
Not even duck-billed platypuses, no kangaroos, no yaks, no camels
or any other king of mammals.
No fish, frogs or birds that sing.' Nothing . . . excepting *man* . . .
what then?
Well if Christ won't have them on his rolls because they've
no immortal soul (though quite frankly I scarce can credit that
he actually ever said it)
Yes, I'll turn my back on heaven and find (with all of them trooping
behind) some place where they will not be banned. *I wonder where*

Ada Tye

BESS

Bess is our dog, our friend and so,
We take her with us wherever we go.

Out in the woods on a fine sunny day
How she loves to run and play.

Up hill, down dale, to and fro,
Hoping that a stick we'll throw.

Down to the river, just for a swim,
Looking round to see if we're in.

A run in the meadow, catching a ball,
I think she likes this most of all.

Mention the car and she's on her feet,
To go for a ride, to her is a treat.

Out in the park for a walk on her lead.
Back in time for her daily feed.

All this she enjoys, and so do we,
Without our Bess, how sad we'd be.

Kathleen Crow

BEN

You followed me one winter's day
You must have been a stray
I took you in and cared for you
Until you passed away.
All the years I had you Ben
You gave me lots of love
A kind and gentle dog
I loved you very much.
Many years have passed now Ben
I shall not forget
You were my own, my darling Ben
My wonderful little pet.

Vicki Tomlin